# First World War
### and Army of Occupation
# War Diary
### France, Belgium and Germany

59 DIVISION
Divisional Troops
470 Field Company Royal Engineers
10 January 1916 - 28 February 1916

WO95/3017/5

The Naval & Military Press Ltd
www.nmarchive.com
**Published in association with The National Archives**

Published by

## The Naval & Military Press Ltd

Unit 10 Ridgewood Industrial Park,

Uckfield, East Sussex,

TN22 5QE England

Tel: +44 (0) 1825 749494

www.naval-military-press.com

www.nmarchive.com

*This diary has been reprinted in facsimile from the original. Any imperfections are inevitably reproduced and the quality may fall short of modern type and cartographic standards.*

© **Crown Copyright**
**Images reproduced by permission of The National Archives, London, England, 2015.**

# Contents

| Document type | Place/Title | Date From | Date To |
|---|---|---|---|
| War Diary | WO95/3017/5 | | |
| Heading | 59 Division 470 Coy Re Formerly 3/1 N Mid Fld Coy RE 1916 Jan-1916 Feb | | |
| Heading | War Diary Of 3/1st North Midland Field Co. R.E. January 1916. | | |
| War Diary | Radlett | 10/01/1916 | 25/01/1916 |
| Heading | War Diary Of 3/1st N.M. Field Coy RE. From February 1st 1916 To February 29th 1916 | | |
| War Diary | Radlett | 17/02/1916 | 28/02/1916 |

WO 95
3017/5

# 59 DIVISION

## 470 COY RE

formerly
3/1 N MID FLD COY RE

1916 JAN — 1916 FEB

CONFIDENTIAL.

WAR DIARY

of

3/1st NORTH MIDLAND FIELD Co. R.E.

January 1916.

Army Form C. 2118.

# WAR DIARY
## or
## INTELLIGENCE SUMMARY.    2/1 N.Md. Field Co. R.E.
*(Erase heading not required.)*

Instructions regarding War Diaries and Intelligence Summaries are contained in F.S. Regs., Part II. and the Staff Manual respectively. Title pages will be prepared in manuscript.

| Place | Date | Hour | Summary of Events and Information | Remarks and references to Appendices |
|---|---|---|---|---|
| | Jan. 1916 | | | |
| Radlett | 10/1/16 | | { Lieut. J.C. Salmon & 12 N.C.O.s & men attached to 179th Brigade at Harpenden for instruction of infantry in field work. | A. |
| | | | Lieut. L. Rotman & 12 N.C.O.s & men attached to 176th Brigade at St Albans for instruction of infantry in field work. | A. |
| | 14/1/16 | | 3 officers and 42 recruits inoculated for enteric fever. | |
| | 25/1/16 | | 2nd Lieut. H. Taylor and 33 men detached to Pirbright to make road in wireless park. | A. |

Signature
Major R.E.
29/1/16

Confidential
War Diary
of
3/1ST H.M. FIELD COY R.E.
From February 1st 1916 to February 29th 1916

(Volume 1)

Army Form C. 2118.

# WAR DIARY
## or
## INTELLIGENCE SUMMARY.
(Erase heading not required.)

2/1 N. Mid. Field Co. R.E.(T)
February 1916

Instructions regarding War Diaries and Intelligence Summaries are contained in F. S. Regs., Part II. and the Staff Manual respectively. Title pages will be prepared in manuscript.

| Place | Date | Hour | Summary of Events and Information | Remarks and references to Appendices |
|---|---|---|---|---|
| | February 1916 | | | |
| Radlett | February 17th | | | |
| " | 19th | | 12 men returned from detached duty at Parkgate | |
| | | | 50 rifles received on loan from 178 Brigade Watford | |
| " | 20th | | 19 men returned from detached duty at St. Albans & Harpenden | |
| " | 21st | | 20 men proceed to St. Albans & Harpenden on detached duty | |
| " | 28th | | O.C. proceeded overseas on a visit to British front in Flanders. | |

Draper
Major & O.C.

www.ingramcontent.com/pod-product-compliance
Lightning Source LLC
Chambersburg PA
CBHW081516160426
43193CB00014B/2710